HIRED!
The Essential Guide To Interview Success

How To Prepare, Perform and Follow Up

S AM W ATERFALL

Obv!ous Publ!sh!ng

Early praise for

"HIRED!
The Essential Guide To Interview Success"

"A useful and practical guide. As someone who has interviewed many hundreds of people throughout my career, I can definitely recommend this short book, it's easy to read and packed full of information. Just looking at those thee golden rules the author presents us with (Prepare, Perform, Follow-up), provides any aspiring candidates with an excellent road map to success."
A. Reilly (UK)

"5 stars. Superb. Quick to read and easy to apply. Sam gets right to the point and comes out firing with fantastic advice for acing your next interview.

What I liked is the fact there are plenty of novel tips and ideas - not the usual dull as dishwater theory. You will learn things you can use today. Once again I can't stress how good it is that the book is quick to read. You can spend more time focusing on preparing and less on reading how to prepare."
Ian Harris (UK)

"Amazing. Got the first job I applied for. Added £16,400 to my salary."
Brand Manager, Kraft Foods (Europe)

"I highly recommend this guide to anyone stressed out about job interviews. I have just finished reading this guide and already feel confident that my job interview on Friday will go very well. The structure of Prepare - Perform - Follow up, plus the what-to-avoid saying and doing advice in each section makes it easy to apply and warns you on common traps people fall into without realising it. It contains tips I never thought are so important at interviews. It is always very helpful to refresh your interview techniques and get a fresh perspective, but this is more than that, it is expert advice delivered at the highest standards and with a good level of detail. I am looking forward to apply live the simple strategies the author suggests. Now I am ready!

Cristina Aldea (Romania & UK)

"Preparing for one of your first ever formal interviews can be a nerve-racking process. Sometimes getting started on the preparation is the most difficult part - how should you structure your research and preparation?

This 'interview doctor' certainly provides a cure, by mapping out, in a very logical manner, how one should go about preparing and thinking about the process. Furthermore, it gives details on how to try to relax and perform during the actual interview. I have no doubts that the 'interview doctor' helped me perform with success during my first-ever formal job interview - and thus helped me land the summer apprenticeship I was applying for. I will definitely go back and have another read before my next one.

All in all, very useful, summed up, to the point and concise! I strongly recommend this to anyone who is the process of preparing for job interviews."

Natasha Treschow (Sweden)

"Light but impactful! I read this book to support my analysis on a project I was working on. Knowing that it was only 46 pages (estimated), I was initially skeptical about whether this book could help. Page-wise, this book is even shorter than my report! However, several pages into the "Introduction", I realized that this book is a concentrate! It's maybe short, but it sure contains all the essence. Less than 30 minutes from the first time I opened the book, I finished reading. And I got all the answers I needed in less than 20 minutes!

Impressed by my own [reading] experience, a few weeks ago I casually cited the golden rules from "Step 1 - Prepare" and "Step 2 - Perform" to a friend who was preparing for a job interview. Guess what? This friend of mine gets hired!

So here's my conclusion of this book: it might look light in appearance, but it is impactful. I would gladly recommend this book to anyone who is preparing for the battle of getting a [dream] job.
Maya Notodisurjo (Indonesia)

"Worked for me. I purchased the book 48 hours before my interview. My last interview was an absolute shambles so I knew I needed some help! I could not answer questions properly and everything went pear shaped, despite thinking I was well prepared. I had been in contact with one of the authors Sam Waterfall before who had helped me with the application process before getting this interview, he suggested this guide so I decided to purchase it. I found it so helpful and a real eye-opener, for example simply putting yourself in the employers shoes, and also the part on 'putting on a show'. I then went on to have a very successful enjoyable interview, I followed all the tips did all the suggested preparing and the employer even let on at the end that they were keen on hiring me, and then I found out the next day I'd officially got the job! So I definitely recommend it!
Ruth Hollah (New Zealand)

Preface

This action-focused *'Essential Guide'* was written for busy Job Seekers who are looking for the winning edge to land the job, but who don't have the time or inclination to read long, drawn-out books on interview skills.

If you are in the job search process, you know the emotions and the pressures that come with it. You know the moments of self-doubt. You know the soul searching. You know the hope.

So when you are invited to an interview you know just how critical it is to make it count.

In this brief guide, Interview Success Coach and Author Sam Waterfall shares his proven methods for acing your performance when it matters most. Dividing your interview approach into three simple steps, he shows you how to Prepare, Perform and Follow Up.

With step-by-step instruction throughout, you'll find tips and guidance you can easily apply without having to spend hours reading long-winded books. The short text you are reading can help you the night before your interview or even if you've downloaded it en route.

Read it. Apply it. And join the thousands who've put The Interview Doctor® tried, tested and proven methods to work to land the job.

Introduction - An Essential Guide

When it comes to Interviews, a few little things can make a very big difference.

This is a short, content-packed guide to help you prepare for interview success.

There are many books with longer, more detailed explanations. But in my experience my Clients prefer this style of shorter action-guide. There's no fluff, no padding, just pure information. And it's short enough to read the night before your interview (or even on the train to your interview) and still be of use... Though I would, of course, recommend giving yourself a little longer to fully prepare and do yourself justice on the day.

How to use this *'Essential Guide'*

It's called *'Essential'* because it contains the concise information you need - just the essentials!

Now you can use it in 2 ways:

1. If you have time to read the detail, you can follow it page-by-page, step-by-step and take action as you go.

2. **If your interview is in the next 48 hours, I recommend you skim through in 10-15 mins noting or highlighting the key actions – then get started!**

"Why are you giving your valuable advice away so cheaply?"

Some people have asked me, *"If your information is so good, why are you virtually giving it away in a book?"*

Well it's a good question, and yes, some of the information which is available in this guide is the same that some of my personal consultancy Clients have paid hundreds of pounds for. But of course, what's here is just the start. When I work one-on-one with my Clients we go into a lot more detail and share the techniques which they can apply to add thousands or even tens of thousands to their annual income.

Good questions, like *"Why are you giving away virtually free advice?"* deserve good answers. So here it is. My hero, author and leading management consultant, Tom Peters says that *"The source of all innovation and progress is p*ssed off people."*

I agree.

While I'm not sure it's the only source, it's a fine one. And it was in fact my immense frustration that led me to start Interview Doctor®. It's my little way of making a difference.

I was so sick of seeing 3 scenarios (see below) that I started my services with a huge ambition – nothing short of **revolutionising the way people present themselves as they apply for jobs.** And in that sense, Interview Doctor® is a cause. I'm starting a movement – teaching people how to properly present themselves in the best light. And my unique approach really works. My Clients are changed people when we're done and they go on to bigger, better paid, more fulfilling jobs – and it often happens faster than they ever imagined possible.

"I started my expert interview and personal branding coaching service with a massive ambition:

To revolutionise the way people present themselves when they apply for jobs."

What led me to start Interview Doctor®?

3 Disasters!

Disaster Scenario 1) Good people constantly getting overlooked

Disaster Scenario 2) The so-called 'Talent Shortage'

Disaster Scenario 3) The wrong people getting hired

Everyday, here in the UK and around the world, superb candidates for jobs are overlooked because they flat out F-A-I-L-E-D to describe themselves appropriately in their interview. That is a travesty!

I'm constantly meeting superb candidates who are so **drastically underselling themselves** that I can promptly boost their confidence and add thousands to their starting salary simply through re-framing their experience. Now please do not misinterpret this. This is not lying. This is not *'massaging the truth'* this is simply explaining what they are capable of in proper business language – the calibre of language which is expected by those in hiring positions.

In the UK (and beyond), we keep hearing of the so-called ***'Talent Shortage'***. Apparently there are too few people with the right skills to support the competitive growth of our economy. While this may be true, the problem could be massively reduced if people knew how to harness and sell the skills – call it ***'Talent'*** if you will – that they have. In short, **job seekers must market themselves!**

And my final frustration: The wrong people getting hired

This is perhaps the worst of all. Whether you are in a small business or a large business, making the wrong hiring decision is a nothing short of a disaster! To say nothing of the financial consequences the disruption to the rest of the team, poor quality work done and vast amounts of time wasted. A wrong decision can set you back weeks vs. your goals. **To help prevent this I'm on a quest for the TRUTH in CVs and interviews.**

So I established Interview Doctor® to combat these scenarios by sharing as widely as possible, the knowledge of how to best market and sell oneself at interview.

How can I help? Why listen to me?

Well, although I studied business for both of my degrees, I was *'in'* business way before. And since then, I've personally navigated the recruitment and selection process for one of the UK's most sought after employers – Procter & Gamble. Likewise, I've successfully passed the process and been hired by other major Blue Chips: Boots The Chemist and Kraft Foods.

In each of these roles I've been a hiring manager alongside my functional remit – fielding CVs, interviewing, hiring and rejecting. Since then as a consultant I've sold my skills and value to major corporations worldwide from South East Asia and the Middle East to the USA, Russia and throughout Europe. In short, I know what it takes and have first hand experience of getting hired into some of the most demanding companies on the planet.

Since starting Interview Doctor® in 2003, I've written CVs and guided the interview success and careers of hundreds of professionals. From CEOs and CIOs with six-figure salaries to FTSE100 Board Directors and from Commercial Professionals and Marketers to Financiers and Medics.

I've worked with people laid off in the recession, mothers returning from maternity leave as well as graduates and students. In every case I've delighted my Clients with a solution which better presents them to their potential employers and boosts their confidence for the interview.

So with Interview Doctor® I combine 3 elements for you:

- I bring my hard-won marketing experience, from marketing products and services.

- I share my tried, tested and proven approaches to winning business relationships.

- And you also benefit from my many years of time served experience crafting individual winning CVs, Cover Letters and Interview Strategies for my personal Clients (FYI I always capitalise 'Clients' because that's how important you are to me).

Bringing you the Insider View – An 'Essential' Guide to Interview Success

Because I've been on the hiring side in multiple companies and because I've helped hundreds of candidates with their CVs and Interview Preparation, I can offer you an unrivalled *'Insider'* View.

In a nutshell here's the best piece of advice I can give you about getting hired:

Stop thinking like a Job Candidate.

Start thinking as if you were the Hiring Manager!

The worst mistakes I've seen marketers make are when they get too *'product focused'* and start to believe they know what's best. Marketers must be *'consumer focused'* and guided by what consumers want. Likewise, job candidates (marketing themselves) must be guided by what the Hiring Managers want.

As US President John F. Kennedy famously espoused during his 1961 Inauguration Speech,

"Ask not what your country can do for you – ask what you can do for your country."

In the same vein...**ambitious job seekers would do well to ask themselves not what their employer can do for them, rather what *they* can do for their *employer*.**

Another, less powerful, but equally appropriate thought is that

"To sell John Brown what John Brown buys you must see the world through John Brown's eyes."

What do I mean?

Put yourself in the position of the Hiring Manager who will read your CV and witness your interview performance. How could you make it easier for that Hiring Manager to take out the information they need from your brief time together in the interview suite?

- Could you give your answers better context to let them know who you are in just a couple of short, high impact sentences?

- Could you improve the quality of your storytelling by adding detail and evidence as you describe events to make it easier for these poor, tired interviewers to understand just how much you have to offer?

- Could you actually talk less and reduce the number of 'umms', 'errs' and junk-filler words you pack-in as you attempt to conceal your nervousness?

Step 1: Prepare

"Failing to plan is planning to fail"

It's the easiest route to avoid this step all together. The good news for you, is that most candidates do exactly that. But you are positioning yourself as a SuperStar Job Candidate. That's what makes it easier to stand out and to get hired. This is your huge advantage over your competition.

These steps will take time. Think of them as an investment in your future. In the days and weeks before your interview make time for this.

If you have a 1-hour interview, you should be spending an absolute minimum of 5 hours preparing.

Find that time. Turn off the TV, get up earlier, stay up later, arrange childcare... Whatever it takes, do it.

Know your 'Why?'

"Why am I attending this interview?"

What are my objectives?

To practice my interview skills? / To understand if this is right for me? / To get the job? / Some combination of these?

Interview Process / Job / Organisational Knowledge

What have I been told by the employer about the selection process?

- Is there a single interview?

- Will you face a panel of interviewers?

- Do you have to do any 'assessment centre' tests like working in a group with other candidates?

- Will a maths or verbal reasoning test be required?

- Might you have to act out a role-play of a situation?

Call ahead if you aren't sure. We don't want surprises on interview day.

What have I been told by the employer about the job?

- Use this knowledge to shape your preparation – study the job description and any lists of skills.

- Identify the key skills / experience they are looking for and work examples of how you demonstrate what they are looking for into every answer you give.

Make sure you know about the organisation / company

- Usually searching their website is a good source of information...

- How are they performing right now? (Sales / Performance / Media attention / Public Opinion)

- What are the challenges they currently face? (Is their whole sector struggling? Are they impacted by macro trends? (e.g. fuel prices / ageing population / health / obesity / Global Warming etc.)

- But don't stop at their website! Trawl the financial press, look what customers are saying about their brands. Are there any activist blogs against them? Any YouTube videos highlighting their malpractice?

- Set out to become an expert – and **don't even consider turning up to an interview without doing 2-4 hours of research**. Do you want this job? If you are serious this is the minimum to do. Your competition will be doing it and if you don't they'll take *your* job.

Know Every Detail on Your CV / Application

Study your CV or the details of the application form you sent. Know all the details about every area.

Think about how you will answer any difficult questions about your CV? (e.g. poor results, short time in jobs, long gaps etc.)

There is no excuse for getting caught out by a question on an obvious gap in your own CV or application. **If you need help developing these interview answers, email our office at info@interviewdoctor.com**.

Prepare for Standard Questions

Most interviews will cover one or more of the following common questions...

"Tell me about yourself"

"Why do you want to leave / did you leave your last job?"

"Why do you think you are well suited to this position?"

"Why do you want to work for us?"

"What skills will you bring to us?"

"What would you say is your biggest weakness?"

"How did you get along with your last manager?"

If one of these comes up, you should be celebrating!

Again, there is no excuse for not having a great answer clear in your head which you can deliver. It is a chance for you to shine! With these questions, as always, be honest. Tough interviewers will probe hard and any lies or embellishment will be revealed.

How should you do it?

Keep answers brief, non-apologetic and to the point. It is a good skill and shows logical and clear thinking if you can give a list of reasons (e.g. There are 2 reasons why I want this job, X and Y).

Prepare for Competency Based Questions

These are designed to probe your experience and your skills vs those pre-determined as appropriate for this job.

These questions tend to follow the format:

"Can you describe an example of a time when you changed somebody's mind about something?"

"Can you tell me about a time you were required to deliver an important result within a tight deadline?"

"How do you deal with people you don't like?"

This 4-step process will generate your winning interview answers:

1. Review the job description and list all of the key skills / behaviours they are looking for.

2. Work through your CV and assign examples of times when you have demonstrated these skills / behaviours.

3. For each skill / behaviour write out your example using the acronym 'C.A.R.' – this is stands for

   Context (outline the situation so the interviewer knows what example you are talking about),

   Actions that YOU took (what you did – so use the word "I" not "We"),

   WOW **Results** (the outcome that YOU achieved – ideally this should have some numbers or specific references to make it easy for the interviewer to understand how good the result was) Remember, WOW Results are the ones that make your interviewer's eyebrows raise in surprise.

4. The key to these questions is responding fully and concisely. 'C.A.R.' will help you do this. Use it – it's the way interviewers are trained to record your answer and making it easy for them will help ease you towards the job!

Prepare for Random Questions

Sometimes an interviewer will ask you a question which will seem odd. This is quite rare, but again, don't let this throw you or unnerve you.

Just be aware you might get an odd question. One good way to prepare is to make sure you are familiar with what is happening in the news right now. You don't have to know every detail, but if there is a burning issue it's good to have an opinion. In this situation the weakest answer is a nervous shrug with *"I don't know really."*

9 Question Answering TIPS:

1. Listen carefully to the question.

2. Answer *that* question, not what you want to talk about.

3. Keep your answer to the point.

4. Don't be modest.

5. Don't exaggerate.

6. Never defend.

7. Never Argue.

8. Avoid slang.

9. Never bad-mouth anyone.

What Will You Wear?

Male or female, this is worth thinking about. And don't leave it to the morning of the interview. Dress appropriately for the role. A dark suit is usually a safe option, combined with an appropriate shirt and, for men, a tie.

The golden rule whether you are a man or a woman is not to let the outfit or the accessories outshine you. They are accessories you are the star! So, go easy on jewellery, bright colours and designer / over-the-top fashionable cuts. Unless the job description specified a specific dress sense, it's safe to assume they are more interested in you than your wardrobe.

This is when it gets really personal. Personal Grooming. You have the choice, to look however you want. Some peoples' 'normal' is someone else's 'radical.' Once again, the idea is to play it conservatively unless the job description specifies otherwise. Keep hair neat and tidy. For women simple make up. For men, research shows a clean-shaven look is more credible and builds greater trust.

Where will the Interview take place?

Make sure you have this all planned out. Some questions you will want to have answered:

- Where are you going?

- Where you will park?

- What train you will catch?

- Do you have cash for a taxi if required?

- Will you need to stay over somewhere if the start is early?

- Do you have a contingency plan if something was to go wrong?

Plan to arrive comfortably ahead of the time you are required to be there.

As well as your map, tickets etc., make sure you have a note of the Name, address and telephone number of your contact.

Obvious as this list may sound, it's not worth compromising your career for lack of thorough planning on the basic logistics of your interview visit.

Phone ahead and confirm your meeting

Almost no one does this!

Set yourself apart again by calling ahead the day before to confirm that you are looking forward to meeting your interviewer at X o'clock at location Y. This sets you up as a class act! It's just a very professional thing to do.

use their name. Instead of saying *"Thank you, Sue"* – they just say *"Thanks"*. Try it together with eye contact – and watch for the smile you get! Now put that to work in your interview.

Dealing with awkward situations or tricky questions

Things can be going well when an interviewer asks a *'tricky'* question. Remember, that they are more interested in **HOW** you deal with this than your actual answer.

If you need time to think – ask for it – say something like *"May I take a moment to think about that, please?"*

If you didn't hear the question properly – say *"Excuse me, would you mind repeating that question for me please?"*

If you didn't understand the question – say so and ask for it to be asked in a different way

Relax and enjoy it!

You will perform best if you are more relaxed. There are only 2 possible outcomes to your interview. You will get told yes or no. If you get told yes – fantastic. If you get told no – learn from it and move on. Nothing terrible will happen. There is no shame in being told no. You just need to say **"Who's next?"** and rapidly move to the next opportunity. When you think of it like this you can see how being overly nervous and on edge can only hinder your chances.

TIP: If you are nervous, place your hands palm-down on your thighs. Try it now. You'll be amazed how difficult it is to be stressed in this sitting position. It also stops you showing any other nervous behaviour like playing with your hair, nose or ears!

Ask Questions

At the end of the interview the *'tables turn'*. After taking maybe an hour of questioning, you will likely get the chance to ask a few questions of your potential employer.

Asking questions at this point is good. It shows confidence and interest and can really build *'chemistry'* with your interviewer. Ask maybe two or three, just don't pull out an A4 pad with a whole page of questions!

Good questions could include:

- *"I'm interested in advancing my career, what role might your successful candidate have risen to in 3 years?"*

- *"What are you personally looking for in a successful candidate?"* This gives you chance to listen and further demonstrate these qualities or skills in the closing stages of the interview.

- *"What are the prospects for development, training, advancement?"*

- *"May I ask what interested you in working at XYZ?"*

- *"What do you enjoy most about working at XYZ?"* This kind of question gives the interviewer chance to talk about him/herself which they will enjoy. You can follow up with other interested questions.

- *"How would you describe the culture of the organisation?"*

- *"From my research on your website I see …. (add relevant fact)…"* and then ask an appropriate question

If you have any kind of restrictive circumstances then this is often a good chance to bring them up if they have not been made clear earlier in your selection process. For example, if you are unable to relocate, or if you need to be able to take time for school or child commitments. Be up front because the interview is a two-way process. The outcome - the employment contract - must work for both sides.

Questions not to ask

Certain questions will send the wrong signal and, in a close-run call between two candidates, they could even reveal something that can cost you the job. Often these might be valid questions, but wait until you've been offered the job before asking:

- *"So how much would I be paid?"*

- *"I've booked two weeks in Spain in August, it'll be ok if I'm off then, won't it?"*

Closing the interview

This is something that is rarely done and can really separate you from the '*also-ran*' candidates.

It is a chance for you to confirm your interest and enthusiasm.

Of course, it is natural for the interviewer to control the process of the interview. However, as you feel things are approaching a conclusion it is really worth saying something like,

"[Interviewer's Name], I've really enjoyed meeting you and having this opportunity to demonstrate my appropriateness for the job. I want to let you know that I'm really interested and feel I could make an excellent contribution here."

If they don't volunteer the next stages of the process, you could say something like,

"[Interviewer's Name], what happens next? / When will you be making a decision?"

STEP 3: Follow Up

"It's never crowded along the extra mile"
– Dr Wayne Dyer

The thank you letter

In many circles the thank you letter is a lost art. It shouldn't be. It is estimated that less than 3% of candidates send a thank you letter to their interviewer.

Why should you?

Quite simply because it sets you apart again and shows you genuinely are a *'class act'*. And if that's not enough for you, it's the perfect way to emphasise your skills and appropriateness for the job. You have asked what they are looking for in their ideal candidate with your questions. This is your chance to re-frame your skills and experience to fit exactly what they are looking for.

Although it's not always possible it's really impressive if this arrives the very next day. If you can get home in time to compose and post it, send it first class for the ultimate finishing touch. Be careful with spellings – don't let yourself down now.

And of course, you need to remember to make sure you have your interviewer's name spelt correctly together with their accurate job title and address. Thank them for their time, mention something you enjoyed about your meeting, re-emphasise your skills **and remember to ask for the job.**

Responding to their communications

When you get offered the job, or invited to the next round of interviews, take a few minutes to congratulate yourself on a job well done! Then reply to them **by return**. This demonstrates you are punctual, decisive and enthusiastic to join them.

Don't resign just yet!

If you are still with your current employer, you should wait to make sure you have all paperwork completed before resigning. Too many people have been caught out this way. Make sure you're not one of them.

Salary negotiation

Job offers usually come with a package. Remember, it is up to you if you want to accept.

Together with a complete range of CV writing and coaching services, interview preparation and presentation skills training, Interview Doctor® provides specific advice on how to maximise your new salary and benefits package. For more detail on any of these services email info@interviewdoctor.com or visit interviewdoctor.com

Closing Thoughts for Your Success

'Mentally flip' the situation!

90% of interview candidates enter the room with a sense of dread, fear and nervousness. If only they took a step back and looked at the entire situation!

There are 2 parties in the interview... those wanting to hire, those wanting to be hired.

So see the interview as what it is – someone looking to hire you! All you have to do is help them to say yes!

Give it your best shot!

James Dean famously advised us all that we should

"Dream as if you'll live forever
and live as if you'll die tomorrow"

I like to think of interviews in the same way. Think big. Dream and picture your success... but don't leave it there...

Be a Hero!

Give it all you have!

Enjoy it!

You have nothing to lose by giving your interview your very best shot.

Go on. How good could you be?

Free Tips And Guidance

For a source of the latest advice on what's working to at interviews, visit

The Interview Doctor® Blog

Interviewdoctor.com/blog

You'll discover the latest tips and Interview Doctor® thinking to accelerate your job search with topics including...

- How to use **LinkedIn.com** to manage your online image and to find your next job faster

- Why your Facebook page could actually be stopping you from landing your dream job

- How to deal with problem details on your CV

- How to stay motivated during your job search

- How to add thousands to your salary when it comes to negotiation time

- And much, much more

About the Author

Interview Doctor® Founder, Sam Waterfall is an entrepreneur, International Marketing Consultant and Speaker. He set up Interview Doctor® – the professional CV writing and interview success coaching service in 2003 to benefit both job candidates and employers.

Sam has personally guided successful career transitions for hundreds of professionals and has influenced and informed many more through his writing, speaking engagements and his blog at interviewdoctor.com. His personal clients have included Fortune 500 and FTSE 100 C-Level and Board Directors as well as graduates and students.

Sam lives in London.

Contact Sam by email on sam@interviewdoctor.com

Also by Sam Waterfall

Available from Amazon on Kindle

The 7 Essential CV Upgrades

... that you can apply in 45mins or less

Created for Job Seekers who sending CVs but getting no replies or interviews.

Telephone Interview Success

How to Prepare, Perform and Follow Up

Created for Job Seekers who have one chance to sell themselves on the phone.

For Your Notes...

For Your Notes...